DIARY OF A
ROBLOX
PRO

Ari
Avatar

T0372163

CASH SPLASH

SCHOLASTIC

First published by Scholastic Australia Pty Limited in 2023.
This edition published by Scholastic in the UK, 2024
1 London Bridge, London, SE1 9BG
Scholastic Ireland, 89E Lagan Road, Dublin Industrial Estate, Glasnevin, Dublin, D11 HP5F

SCHOLASTIC and associated logos are trademarks,
and/or registered trademarks of Scholastic Inc.

Published by Scholastic Australia in 2023.
Text copyright © Scholastic Australia, 2023.
Illustrations copyright © Scholastic Australia, 2023.
Cover design by Hannah Janzen.
Internal design by Paul Hallam.

ISBN 978 0702 33370 5

Printed and bound in Great Britain by Clays Ltd, Elcograf S.p.A
Paper made from wood grown in sustainable forests and other controlled sources.

1 3 5 7 9 10 8 6 4 2
www.scholastic.co.uk

MIX
Paper | Supporting
responsible forestry
FSC® C018072

SATURDAY AFTERNOON

"Ah, **BRAIN FREEZE!**" I cried, clutching my head as the cold from my chocolate thickshake hit my brain.

"You need a **BRAIN** to get brain freeze," Zeke joked, throwing a potato chip at me.

"Ha ha. So, where's this shop we have to go to?" I asked, looking around the food court of the shopping centre.

"Down on the bottom level," Jez said. "It's got all kinds of art supplies, so we'll be able to find what we need."

Jez, Zeke and I needed to create a model solar system out of craft supplies for a school group assignment. Our plan was to paint foam balls and hang them from wire to string across the room.

Jez, of course, had figured out the maths to create an exact scaled model. This meant that all of our planets would be accurately scaled in size.

Jez sipped her bubble tea, then scooped up a jelly to pop into her mouth.

"Did you hear that the new **AIR PUMP 3000s** have just released?" Zeke said. "I want to go check them out."

"Awesome!" I said.

"Probably costs like a **MILLION** Robux, though," Jez said.

She was probably right. Air Pump sneakers were the coolest shoes around. The only avatar I knew who got the new release editions was Trip from school. He's a total bully, but also happens to be the mayor's son and gets whatever he wants.

"Zeke, your birthday is coming up. Maybe you could get a pair?" I said. "You'd be the coolest avatar at school."

Zeke shrugged. "I doubt my parents could afford them, but an avatar can dream!"

We finished our after-school snacks and threw our rubbish into the bins. But instead of going downstairs to the craft supply store, we took the escalator up to the Air Pump store.

Even from a distance, we could see the large crowd of young avatars gathered around the shop window. As we approached, we heard them oohing and aahing.

"So **EPIC!**" one avatar said.

"How cool are the colours?" another added.

"I bet they make you jump really

high, too," another said. " I'd be an obby **PRO** if I had those."

Zeke, Jez and I elbowed our way to the window and looked in. There, sitting on a little podium, was the **COOLEST** pair of sneakers I'd ever seen in my life.

"Let's go in and check them out,"
Jez said.

So we walked inside the store to
get a closer look. There was no
way the store would let avatars
touch or try them on—not when
they were still limited edition. But
the avatar working there was
doing a demo.

"So here it is," he announced. "The
AIR PUMP 3000!"

The crowd was silent with awe.

"And check this out," the store

assistant said, bending his knees. He then jumped, **SHOOTING** up as high as the store ceiling.

"WHOA!" we all breathed.

"With these shoes, you'll be an obby pro in no time," he said as he landed softly back on the ground. "And that's not all! The rocket power mode will make you run as fast as a cheetah," he added.

He burst forward, running through the store at **LIGHTNING** speed.

The crowd erupted into cheers.

"I've never wanted something so much in my life!" I said, bouncing up and down. "I'd literally trade anything for a pair of these."

"ANYTHING?" Jez challenged, raising an eyebrow.

"Yep," I said resolutely.

"Like, your family? Your dog? Your *friends?*" she challenged.

I hesitated.

"Oh, thanks a lot, Ari!" she yelled, offended.

"No, no, of course not you guys,"
I said hurriedly.

"You don't sound very convincing,
Ari," Zeke jumped in, narrowing
his eyes.

"Clear the way, clear the way,"
an obnoxious voice called from
behind us. We didn't need to turn
around to know who it was.

TRIP.

"The mayor is here, clear the
way," Trip yelled, as the crowd
parted around him.

Trip and his mum, the mayor of Blockville, walked to the front of the store.

"Excuse me," his mum said to the store assistant. "My son would like to try on the new Air Pump 3000 shoes."

The assistant looked at them, knowing that he was under strict instructions to only let avatars try them on if he was sure they'd buy them.

"I'm the mayor," Trip's mum added, sensing his hesitation.

"Of course, ma'am," the assistant said. He then turned to Trip. "What size, sir?" he asked politely.

Everyone stared as Trip was measured up for his shoes. Then the store assistant brought out a shoebox and opened it to reveal the **SHINING** new shoes.

Trip tried them on. He jumped up and almost hit the roof, then he ran around the store, knocking over several avatars.

"How are they, darling?" his mum asked.

"They're OK," Trip said, scrunching up his nose. "I thought they'd be **BETTER.**"

"Do you not want them?" the mayor asked her son.

"Eh, I guess I'll take them," Trip said, shrugging. "If they're trash I'll just give them to the dog."

UUUUGGGH!

"I can't *stand* Trip," I whispered to Jez and Zeke.

After his mum swiped her credit card at the counter, her and Trip then walked out of the store with his new shoes in a sparkling Air Pump bag.

UNFAIR.

SUNDAY MORNING

> **@t3ch_qu33n:** Ari! Zeke! Portal alert!

The words flashed across my gaming screen. I didn't even need to check the username to know who sent that message.

Jez.

Jez is a tech whizz. And she's always looking for **PORTALS** into parallel universes and other dimensions. I never believed they existed until we finally found one. And that almost ended in us becoming **ZOMBIES,** so I wasn't too keen on finding another one.

@zekeobbypro77: IRL?

@t3ch_qu33n: Yes, REAL LIFE!

Zeke's username flashed as he typed out another reply, but he must have deleted it because the flashing stopped without any message coming through. I bet

he was thinking the same thing
I was—that he wasn't in the mood
to run away from monsters or
zombies on a Sunday morning.

Jez's words **FLASHED** up on the
screen.

> @t3ch_qu33n: Come on, plz???

I quickly typed out a response and
hit send before I had time to think
any more about it.

> @Me: OK

@t3ch_qu33n: EPIC!
Park. 15 mins.

Switching off my device, I walked over to my wardrobe. I pulled out my old sneakers and put them on. A surge of **JEALOUSY** ran through me as I looked at the scruffy shoes. They were so not cool. Totally something a **NOOB** would wear.

I shook my head to get rid of the thought and stood up. Then I went downstairs to where my mum and dad were drinking their morning coffee.

"Where are you going?" Mum asked.

"Can I go meet Zeke and Jez at the park?" I asked.

"Yes, that's OK. Just make sure you're home for lunch," Dad said.

Smiling at them in thanks, I wandered out the door.

Luckily I didn't need to walk far, since the park was super close to my house. When I arrived, I could see Zeke and Jez already standing over by the slides. Jez was holding her tablet and was **FRENZIEDLY** navigating her portal tracking system.

"Sup, Ari!" Zeke said, giving me a high five.

"What'd you find?" I asked Jez, leaning in to look at her screen.

"According to my **PORTAL TRACKER** app, the portal is somewhere in that direction," she said, pointing to the bushland behind the park.

"Should we go check it out?" Zeke asked.

I shrugged.

"Come on! Don't be a **CHICKEN**," she teased.

We walked to the back of the park and jumped over the low wire fence. The dirt track snaked steeply downwards into thick bushland. It was darker down here and I could hear the rush of the creek at the bottom of the hill.

"Down this way," Jez said, following the track further down.

We got to the bottom of the hill, where the creek ran. It hadn't rained much lately, so it was pretty shallow with a lots of rocks peeking up through the surface of the water.

"What do you reckon is in the portal this time?" I asked

nervously, the image of zombies still fresh in my mind.

"Could be anything," Jez said. "Some theories state that portals lead to other dimensions. That's probably correct, considering the zombies we saw last time. Another theory is that they lead to other planets. I'm not sure about that one. And then there's the **PARALLEL UNIVERSE** theory ..."

"The what?" Zeke asked.

"Parallel universe. It's like our

world, but slightly **DIFFERENT,"**
Jez said.

"Different how?" Zeke asked.

"Like, the trees are made of
candy?" I asked hopefully.

"Or there's no such thing as
school?" Zeke added.

Jez **LAUGHED.** "Maybe! Who
knows? But I bet the Jez in the
candy tree world loves it there."

"What do you mean, the Jez in
the candy tree world?" I asked.

"Are you saying there would be another you in that universe?"

"Most likely!" she said. "I mean, if the universe is parallel, which shares similarities to our world, then there's every chance we could all exist over there, too."

I swallowed hard. It was kind of cool but also kind of **CREEPY** to think about. What would parallel-Ari be doing right now?

We walked deeper into the bushland and the canopy above us became thicker. The air darkened and I could smell the damp soil around the creek, musty and earthy.

Jez suddenly stopped, silently holding up her hand to point at something ahead.

We crept forward slowly and then gazed around the thick gum tree Jez pointed to.

There, in front of us, was a pulsing purple light, shimmering amongst the dark trees.

"A PORTAL," Jez breathed,

her eyes widening in excitement.

We stalked up to the glowing
portal, which tinted our faces
with its faint light. Jez gingerly
reached out her hand.

Jez gently touched the light.
The low **HUMMING** of the portal
glitched and changed frequency,
then returned to normal as she
pulled her hand back.

"What now?" I whispered
urgently. "What if there are more
ZOMBIES?" My tummy felt
like it was full of butterflies.

"Well, who's brave enough to go through it?" Zeke said. "There could be anything on the other side."

We stood, basking in the glow of the portal's light, contemplating what to do next. But before we could do anything, a **HAND** suddenly burst through.

"AAAAAAGGGH!"

SUNDAY MORNING — A BIT LATER

We **SCREAMED** as the hand quickly retracted back into the portal.

"Is it a zombie?" I stammered.

We stood back and watched with wide eyes.

Then the arm burst through again. But it didn't look like it belonged to a monster or a zombie. It looked like a regular avatar arm.

"I don't think its a zombie world . . ."
Jez said carefully.

A head then appeared next to the
arm on our side of the portal.

"Whoa, that's **EPIC!**" the head
yelled with . . . my voice?

Zeke looked from the head
sticking out of the portal to me.

"Wait, what?" he exclaimed.

I stood up straighter to inspect

the head. The avatar on the other side looked just as shocked as I felt. It was like looking in a mirror—he was my exact copy!

"Ari—" Jez began.

"Yeah?" the head and I said at the same time.

"Are . . . are you me? From a parallel universe?" I stammered.

"COOL!" the head yelled, jumping completely through the portal and popping out onto our side.

"Whoa, he looks just like you but with a lot more *bling*," Jez laughed.

I looked at Other-Ari. He was dressed in a **GOLDEN** suit jacket, which shimmered in the light of the portal. And on his feet were—

"AIR PUMP 3000s!"

Zeke yelled.

Other-Ari shrugged. "No big deal. These aren't even my coolest shoes."

He then looked me up and down, inspecting my worn sneakers. He **GRIMACED** as he looked at my clothes.

"Aw, man! Am I *poor* in this universe?" he said.

His voice sounded like mine, but it also didn't sound like mine. There was something about it that wasn't right. It was more high-pitched and forceful and ... **DEMANDING.**

"I'm not poor," I said, defensively.

Other-Ari then turned to my friends, noticing them for the first time since jumping through the portal. His eyes widened.

"You recognize us!" Jez said. "Are Jez and Zeke in your universe, too?" she asked excitedly.

Other-Ari's cheeks went pink. "Uh, no, no, they're not. Never heard of

you. Never even seen you before,"
he said quickly.

Jez and Zeke looked disappointed.

"So, what's life like in your world?"
I asked Other-Ari, curiously.

"Aw, you know. I mean, I do
pretty well for myself. Live in
a sweet pad with everything I
want, really," he said, then added
with a wink, "I'm kind of a **BIG
DEAL** over there."

I winced. Other-Ari sounded like a
bit of a show-off.

"I've got a tennis court, pool, private obby course, a pet lion, a crocodile and an entire herd of dragons, a Robux bank vault—you know, all that stuff. How about you?" he asked.

"Ah, kinda the same," I said.

Jez and Zeke smothered a laugh.

"I just meant that I live a normal life. I have my mum and dad and sister, Ally—"

"You live with Ally?" Other-Ari interrupted.

I nodded. "You don't live with your sister?"

He shook his head but didn't elaborate. Maybe Ally didn't exist in his world.

"I like **OBBIES** and I have a dog named Coda. That's about it," I said, shrugging. "And school, I guess."

"Wait, you go to school?" Other-Ari asked. For someone so cool, he seemed pretty interested in my life.

I nodded.

"What's it like? Do you have heaps of **FRIENDS?** Do you play tricks on the teacher?" he asked with wide eyes.

"You don't have school in your universe?" Zeke asked. "Dude, I want to live in your world!"

"Nah, mate, we have school. I just . . . don't need to go," he said quickly.

I frowned.

"Mate, I just had the most **EPIC** idea," Other-Ari said. "How'd you like to live in my world for a bit?"

"What do you mean?" I asked.

"Let's **SWAP** worlds! Just for a few days. I can go to your school and live in your world, and you can live in mine! We'll swap back on Tuesday," he said, excitedly.

A wave of uncertainty washed over me. "I—I dunno," I stammered.

"Your friends here can show me where you live and teach me how to be you so that your family don't suspect," he added.

"What about me?" I asked. "I don't even know where you live on the other side of that portal."

"My friend is on the other side. He knows I came through. He's really loyal—if you explain everything to him, he'll help you and keep your **SECRET,**" Other-Ari said.

"Maybe . . ." I said, thinking.

"You can use my private obby and—" Other-Ari stopped and took off his shoes. "Here, you can have **THESE!**"

42

My eyes lit up at the sight of the Air Pump 3000s.

"Ari, are you sure?" Zeke asked.

"I mean, it's just a few days, right? What could go wrong?" I said, reaching out to take the shoes.

Jez checked her Portal Tracker app. "I guess a few days can't hurt. This says the portal will be open until midday on Tuesday," she said.

"AWESOME!" Other-Ari cheered. "It's decided then. We'll need to swap clothes."

We hurriedly swapped our clothes over and once he was dressed in my old gear, not even my mum would recognize him as an **IMPOSTER.**

I looked down at the golden suit jacket and Air Pump 3000s I was wearing. The shoes felt amazing— like walking on a cloud!

"So, we meet back here at the park on Tuesday morning, 8 am sharp," Other-Ari said. "Is there anything I need to know about what's happening in your world between now and then?"

"Oh, yeah, I've got a Maths test on Monday. How are you at Maths?" I asked.

"I'm awesome at it! I get a lot of practice counting my **MONEY,**" he said.

It wasn't very convincing. "Is there anything I need to know about you?" I asked.

Other-Ari thought for a minute. "Yep, you have a meeting on Monday. Just go with Option A."

"What's Option A?" I asked.

"Doesn't matter—all you need to know is that when they ask you what you want to do, always go with Option A," he said with a serious face. "It's very important that our decisions are consistent."

I shrugged and nodded. "You got it, mate!" I was beginning to get excited.

We **FIST-BUMPED** as Other-Ari stood next to my friends. Zeke and Jez looked a little unsure but forced smiles.

"Be careful, Ari," Jez said.

"Make sure you come back—that other life sounds pretty sweet," Zeke said. "Don't forget about us."

I smiled at him. "Never. See you Tuesday!" I said.

Then I leapd into the portal.

SUNDAY—
A FEW
SECONDS
LATER

A haze of purple swirled around my face, making me dizzy. It felt like I was caught in a tornado, electric static making the hairs on my arm stand up. Suddenly, a pulse of wind launched me forwards, **PUSHING** me out the other side of the portal. I tumbled head first onto grass on the other side.

"OOF!"

"Are you OK, Master Ari?" a voice said from above me.

I quickly stood up and dusted myself off. A man stood in front of me dressed in a grey suit. He had long legs and a pointy face, with a thin moustache above his upper lip.

"I, uh—" I stammered.

"Have you hit your head, Master Ari? You seem confused!" he said, leaning in to look at my eyes.

"Who are you?" I asked.

The man looked alarmed.
"It's me, Master Ari. Gerald.
Your **BUTLER,** remember?"

I have a butler?! I thought for
a moment. Could I tell him about
the switch? Other-Ari said I could
trust him, but I didn't know who
this man was.

I changed my stunned look to
a confident smile—the kind that
Other-Ari would make.

"I'm just messing with you, mate!"
I said, **SLAPPING** him on the back.

His face melted into relief.

"Oh, yes, jolly good, Master Ari,"
he laughed. "Did you see
anything through the portal?"

"Nah, just some boring **LAME**
world," I said quickly.

"As I said it would be!"
Gerald chuckled. "It's nearly
lunchtime. Shall we head back
to the estate?"

Estate?!

"Uh, that would be . . . grand.
Thank you, Gerald," I said.

Gerald frowned slightly. Then he laughed again. "You're still being funny with me, aren't you, Master Ari?"

"Uh, yeah!" I quickly agreed.

"Come on, then," he said, gesturing for me to walk ahead.

I suddenly realized I had no idea where I was meant to be going.

"You lead the way," I said, **FAKING** confidence.

Gerald smiled and led us up the

bush track. If this world was like my world, we should be heading towards the park.

We broke through the trees and there in front of me was—

"Where's the **PARK?!**" I cried.

"I beg your pardon?" Gerald asked, turning towards me.

Instead of a beautiful park with play equipment, paths for scooters and grassy picnic areas, there was a barren plot of dirt filled with broken-down, rusted cars.

"Uh, I just . . ." I stammered. "Do you remember when this was a park, Gerald?" I asked carefully, hoping I wasn't giving myself away.

"Ah, yes, Master Ari, I do. It was such a waste of space, wasn't it? Much better as a dumping ground for the rusted old cars you don't drive anymore!" he said. But as he looked around the ugly plot, his eyes looked sad.

I bowed my head, embarrassed.

We walked through the abandoned lot and reached

the street. There, in front
of us, was a shining golden
MOTORBIKE, with a small
cart attached to the side.

"WHOA!" I said.

"What is it?" Gerald asked, putting on his helmet and cramming himself into the side car.

"I mean—uh—I forgot how **COOL** my bike is!" I muttered. "But, Gerald, I was thinking, do you want a turn at driving it?"

"Me?" Gerald asked, shocked.

I really hoped Gerald would say yes. I had no idea how to drive a motorbike and no idea where we were going!

"Oh, Master Ari! That's the kindest

thing you've ever offered me,"
he said, tears in his eyes. "You
know how much I love motorbikes.
I never thought I'd see the day—"

"No sweat," I said, putting on my
own helmet. "Hop on!"

Gerald beamed as he moved onto
the motorbike, while I jumped into
the sidecar.

Gerald revved the throttle and
we **BURST** out onto the road.
Gerald may have looked super
conservative, but he was driving
like a **PRO!** We weaved through

the streets, taking corners at
speed and racing down the hills.
I held on tightly, my knuckles
turning white on the sidecar's
golden handlebars.

The sights around me passed by
in a blur of colour as we sped
on. But when I was able to catch
a glimpse of Blockville, the town
looked so **DIFFERENT** to
the one back in my own universe.
The streets here were lined with
factories spewing black smoke up
into the air. Many of my friends'
houses were gone. I wondered
where they all lived.

Once we passed through the factory district, we turned the corner and a huge sprawling **MANSION** came into view. It was bigger than my entire school and sat up on a hill, overlooking all of Blockville.

My jaw dropped. That couldn't possibly be my house, could it?

SUNDAY—
LUNCHTIME

The motorbike climbed the hill
and approached large gates at
the top. As we neared, the gates
slowly opened, welcoming us into
the estate. My estate!

After getting out of the sidecar,
I followed Gerald up the front
steps and into the mansion's grand
entrance. The foyer alone was
completely **EPIC!** There was
a massive staircase, with a slide
running down one side.

Gerald led me past the staircase
and through to an adjoining
room. It was full of couches and
beanbags and lining the walls
were huge TVs all hooked up with
gaming units.

"COOL," I breathed.

"Would you like lunch now, or would you prefer to do a spot of **GAMING** first, Master Ari?" Gerald asked.

"Oh, whatever works for you," I shrugged. "I can help make pizza?"

Gerald stared at me with his mouth slightly open.

"Uh . . . well, the kitchen staff are preparing the **BURGER** you asked for. But if you've changed your mind, I can tell them to throw it in the bin and start again?" Gerald suggested.

I **LAUGHED** until I saw he was completely serious.

"Burgers are great," I said quickly.

Gerald frowned slightly and shook his head.

"Shall I bring your meal to your room, Master Ari, or would you like to eat here?" he asked, gesturing to the dining room we were walking towards.

I realized I had no idea where 'my' room was, so I quickly answered that the dining room was perfect. Gerald frowned again, but nodded politely and left the room. Maybe Other-Ari didn't eat here very often.

I sat down at the long table and looked around. Photos hung on the walls all around the room. I almost **CHOKED** when I saw who was in them.

One had Other-Ari posing with popstar Brickey Sparkles. Another had him standing with Olympic gold medallist, Kurt Blockstill. In another, Other-Ari was sitting on a film set next to super famous actor, The Block.

How on earth did Other-Ari know
all these **CELEBRITIES?**
He really was a big deal here.

A few minutes later, Gerald came
back with a platter balanced on
his palm. Resting on top of the
platter was the most epic burger
I had ever seen. He placed it
in front of me and my mouth
WATERED. It had everything I like
on it—beef, cheese, bacon, lettuce
and tomato. And some ketchup, too.

NOM, NOM, NOM!

Before I took I bite, I noticed
Gerald still **HOVERING**
over me.

"Are you joining me?" I asked.

"Wh—what do you mean, sir?"
he stuttered

"Where's your burger?" I said.

"Oh. I was going to have it later.
After you finished," Gerald said
slowly.

"Nah, go and get it. I don't want
to eat alone!" I said.

Gerald stared at me for a few seconds then disappeared back through the kitchen doors.

He returned shortly after with his own burger. I pulled out the chair next to me and motioned for him to sit down.

"You want me to eat with you?" he asked.

I nodded.

Seeing Gerald's **SHOCK** made me realize that maybe Other-Ari didn't dine with his staff very much.

"May I be so bold as to say something?" he asked.

"Yeah, of course," I said around a mouthful of burger.

"I just wanted to say **THANK YOU.**"

"Uh, why?" I asked.

"Oh, you know. It's just . . . letting me ride your motorbike and dine with you? Well, it's an honour, sir," Gerald said with sparkling eyes.

"Dude, there's one thing I'm going to have to insist on," I said.

Gerald coughed gently and sat up straighter. "Of course, sir."

"Stop calling me 'sir'!" I said, breaking into a smile.

"Ah, you prefer 'Master Ari'. I understand," Gerald said quickly.

"NAH," I interrupted. "Just Ari from now on, OK?"

Gerald hesitated, but then nodded. As he started to eat his burger, I swear I saw a tear in his eye.

SUNDAY AFTERNOON

After lunch, I told Gerald that

I just wanted to chill on my own.

What I didn't tell him was that

I just wanted to **EXPLORE**

the estate without raising suspicion.

I began my exploration by looking

for my—I mean, Other-Ari's—room.

I travelled up the stairs, along

the hallways and checked in on

a stack of rooms. There seemed

to be a room for everything—

a candy room, a gaming room,

a room with rock climbing all up the walls, a trampoline room, a music room—it was **EPIC.**

Finally, I entered a large room which was definitely Other-Ari's bedroom.

Inside, there was a massive **KING-SIZED** bed topped with a fluffy blanket and a mountain of pillows. There was a huge TV screen on the wall opposite the bed and a computer set up on a large desk.

All over the walls were signed

posters of the biggest movies and games around.

I walked up to the closet and opened the doors.

WHHHHHOOOOOOAAAAA!

The walk-in closet was bigger than my entire bedroom was back home! It was lined with rows and rows of designer clothes, and a tower of shelves held dozens of pairs of the most expensive shoes around. The Air Pump 3000s I was wearing suddenly didn't seem so cool anymore.

I reached up to grab a pair that looked particularly epic. I read the label on the shelf.

"ROCKET 6000."

Rocket?

I pulled off the Air Pumps and slipped on the Rockets. They were pretty comfy. I noticed a small circle on the top of the shoes, which looked like a tiny button. I leant down and pressed it.

All of a sudden, **FLAMES** shot out of the soles of the shoes and

I hovered a few feet above the ground.

"WHOA!" I yelled, wobbling in the air.

I quickly gained my balance and started to fly around the bedroom.

"This is **AWESOME!! WOOHOO!**" I yelled.

I looked behind me to see if my friends were watching, but the empty room reminded me that I was on my own in this world. My smile faded. It was less cool without anybody to share it with.

I tried to forget about it and kept playing with the Rocket shoes, whizzing up and down the hallway until I was **EXHAUSTED.** I then changed back into the Air Pump 3000s and went out to explore the other rooms.

Once on the ground floor, I peeked my head into a huge room—it was almost as big as a gymnasium. And it was filled entirely with **OBBY CHALLENGES.** Zeke would have loved this!

The obby was massive. There were ladders, platforms and laser lights (which didn't actually blast you—they were just for practice).

I climbed up the first ladder I saw, then **JUMPED** from block to block. Some of the blocks were spinning around in circles, and

I had to time it perfectly to land on them without falling. It took me ages to get through the whole obby without falling off. Zeke would have blitzed it in one go because he's an obby pro! I so badly wished he was here right now.

After finishing the obby, I went outside to check out the grounds. It was **EPIC!** I had jumping castles, farm animals and park equipment. There was even a huge pool with a waterfall and waterslide! I then came across a huge outdoor building with massively high walls and a

large dome roof. Going inside,
I discovered that Other-Ari had
an entire herd of **DRAGONS**
in there! One of them flew right
up to me and hovered above me.
He leaned in and **SNIFFED** me
before flying away, confused as
to who I was.

SNIFF
SNIFF

The dragons made me nervous,
but then I noticed something shiny
hanging from a hook on the wall.
Above it was a sign that read
"DRAGON WHISTLE".
I wondered if it was like the dog
training whistle we had for Coda.

I grabbed the whistle and blew
it. The dragon immediately **RACED**
over to me like an obedient puppy.
Cool! After a minute or two,
I guess he decided to trust me,
because he bent down low and
waited for me to climb onto his
back. I sat on his shoulders and
held onto his neck. With another

blow of the whistle, the dragon **SHOT** up into the air and flew in circles around the pen. The other dragons chased us playfully as we ducked and weaved through the air. It was so **AWESOME,** but it was such a shame Jez wasn't there—she loved rare animals. Once we landed, I slipped the dragon whistle into my pocket.

After leaving the dragons, I was gassed. I decided to go back up to my room for a nap.

SUNDAY — LATE AFTERNOON

Once in my room, I immediately flopped onto my bed. It was **EXHAUSTING** being Other-Ari! Rolling onto my side, I saw something poking out of the bedside table drawer. Sitting up, I opened the drawer and pulled out a photo. It was **JEZ** and **ZEKE!** Other-Ari had his arms around two avatars, who looked exactly like my best friends. That was totally weird though, because Other-Ari said he'd never seen anyone that looked like Jez and Zeke before. Why would he **LIE?**

"Sir—I mean, Ari?" a voice called from the door. It was Gerald.

"Oh, hi, Gerald," I said.

"Where would you like your afternoon snack today?" he asked.

"Maybe the games room. Am I allowed to eat in there?" I asked.

Gerald laughed. His face then turned to concern when he realised I wasn't kidding.

"Well, yes, of course," he said **FROWNING.**

"Gerald," I started slowly. I had to work out how to ask this question without giving myself away. "I found this," I continued, holding up the photo.

"Oh, yes. Would you like me to get

rid of it?" Gerald asked. "You said you don't want any pictures of those . . . what do you call them? **NOOBS?**"

I shook my head. It seemed like Other-Ari and the Jez and Zeke look-alikes weren't friends anymore.

"Nah, it's okay. But, do you think one day, we might . . . I dunno . . . hang out again?" I asked carefully.

Gerald tilted his head to the side. "Ari, you said you never wanted to see them again. Or rather, they never wanted to see you again."

What did Other-Ari do?

"Do you think they'd ever . . .
I dunno, **FORGIVE ME**
and we could patch things up?"
I prodded.

"Forgive you?" Gerald said,
incredulously. "It's those avatars
that should be asking you
to forgive them! They were
JEALOUS of your wealth
and refused to hang out with you
anymore. They *blocked* you."

They certainly didn't sound like
the Jez and Zeke from my world.

Then something else occurred to me. Other–Ari had no friends, but what about his family?

"And my parents and sister . . ." I began casually, trying to sound cool. "Will they be . . . visiting this week?"

Gerald looked completely confused.

"Your family hasn't seen you in years, sir. They still live outside of town. They haven't tried to contact you since you became rich," Gerald said. He then took a step towards me, looking concerned.

"Are you all right, Ari? You are acting very **STRANGELY.**"

"Uh, yeah, sorry, just tired. I mean, of course I know my family lives out of town. I just wondered if they'd tried to call or something," I said sadly.

"No, sir. They were worse than your friends, trying to use your wealth for themselves. And that **GREEDY** sister of yours . . ." Gerald trailed off, shaking his head.

Gerald then turned and walked out of the room, gently shutting the door behind him and leaving me alone. As I lay there, I stared down at the photo of Zeke and Jez. I couldn't stop thinking about how **HORRIBLE** this world was. All the people I knew and loved in my world were absolutely terrible in this place. It made me want to go home.

Something suddenly **FLUTTERED** in through the window. I turned to see a paper plane cruise across the room and land gently on the carpet.

WEIRD.

I got off my bed and bent down
to pick it up, then looked out the
window to see who had thrown it.
Two shadowy figures with hoods
pulled up over their heads slipped
away between the hedges.

Curious, I unfolded the plane.

Meet us in industrial complex B
by the old park in an hour.
—Two friends.

I **FROWNED.** It sounded like
Other-Ari didn't have any friends.
So who was this note really
from? I briefly thought about

telling Gerald. Other-Ari said
he was trustworthy, but I wasn't
sure what he would do. Maybe
I should just ignore the note? But
something **NIGGLED** at me. It was
the final line. Two **FRIENDS.**
I sure could have used those at
that moment. So I decided to go.

SUNDAY EVENING

One hour later, the sun was beginning to set, so I told Gerald that I wanted to go for a ride on my **HOVERBOARD.** Yep, a hoverboard! Slipping on a helmet, I jumped on to the board and left the estate.

Even on the rough terrain, the ride was smooth. The board hovered about a foot above the ground, allowing it to **GLIDE** over the pathway effortlessly.

Within minutes I had made it to the dark and quiet industrial complex. I looked around.

"HELLO?" I called out nervously.

My voice echoed off the big factory buildings.

I saw a **FLASH** of movement.

"Is someone there?" I yelled.

"SSSSHH!" a voice hissed back.

A hand emerged from the shadows and beckoned me closer.

I swallowed **NERVOUSLY** as I hesitantly tiptoed over.

"Who—who's there?" I whispered.

Two hooded figures stepped into the light. They **PULLED DOWN** their hoods to reveal . . .

"Zeke! Jez!" I **YELLED,** almost giving them a hug. But then I remembered that they weren't my Zeke and Jez. These two were the ones who had totally blocked Other-Ari.

"Ari, I can't believe you came, mate," Zeke said, putting his arm out for a **FIST BUMP.** "We've tried so many times to reach you, but you've been ignoring our messages."

I looked at my friends. Even though they weren't my actual friends, there was something so

familiar in their eyes. Despite
what Gerald said, there was
no way these guys would have
blocked Other-Ari. So, I decided
to **TRUST** them and told them
everything. I told them about
the portal, about the swap with
Other-Ari, about my universe and
theirs. And that I was only going
to be here until tomorrow.

"Whoa, that's an epic story," Jez
breathed.

"No wonder you came. Our Ari
would never have come to see us,"
Zeke added sadly.

"Guys, I have to know what happened. Gerald told me you guys blocked Ari because you were jealous of his wealth. And that his family abandoned him," I said.

Zeke and Jez shook their heads.

"He's a **LIAR,**" Jez said. "And we've been trying to tell you—uh, our Ari—for more than a year. But he's been brainwashed."

"What actually happened?" I asked.

Jez took a **DEEP BREATH.** "It went down like this . . ."

Ari won
a competition
run by a huge
corporation.

The prize was
a **MILLION** Robux.
He couldn't believe it when he won.
At first, he was super generous
and was helping his friends and
giving it away to charity. He
bought the estate up on the hill,
but was still coming to school.

But his prize money came with
CONDITIONS. The
corporation made him buy into
their company which made him,

and them, more money. They used him in their **DODGY DEALS,** knowing that nobody would suspect treachery from a kid. As the company got richer, Ari also got richer, so he kept doing it. But when he sold the school, we told him he was being used. He got **MAD.** The president of the company isolated Ari and spread lies about us and his family.

The company continued to use Ari as their puppet and kept doing dodgy things like replacing our parks with factories, putting Blockville businesses out of work and even built oil rigs on the reef.

Ari became so **POWERFUL** that nothing could stop him. And nobody could talk to him to tell him he was being used."

I frowned. It all sounded so wrong.

"And tomorrow is the final nail in the Blockville coffin," Zeke said. "Our Ari is supposed to sign a document to **SELL BLOCKVILLE!** The whole town will finally be one big dirty factory where nobody can live."

"Ari wouldn't do that!" I protested.

"Ever heard of **OPTION A?**" Jez asked.

I remembered back to what Other-Ari had said. Choose Option A.

That must have been the option
to sell Blockville!

"But I haven't even met this
company president," I said. "If he's
so powerful, why haven't I met him
in the mansion?"

Jez and Zeke looked **CONFUSED.**
"But you have. We saw you with
him earlier," Zeke said.

I shook my head. They must have
been mistaken.

Zeke put his hand on my shoulder.
"Ari, the president is Gerald."

SUNDAY EVENING — DARK

"So, you figured it out," a menacing voice said from behind us. We gasped. It was Gerald. And he was holding a **TASER** weapon.

"You **WON'T** get away with this!" I yelled. "I'm going to tell Other-Ari what you've done and how you've used him! And he'll vote to get rid of you from the company and restore Blockville to what it was before you corrupted everything!"

Gerald let out a sinister **CACKLE.**
"I don't think so, little avatar!
I sent Ari over to your universe
so that once we sell Blockville in
this world, we can go over there
and steal yours, too!"

"NO!"

Gerald held up the taser weapon.
"If you three don't want to be
zapped into a world of pain,
I suggest you do what I say.
GET INSIDE!" he said, nodding to
the open door of the factory.

We had no choice.

Walking inside, Gerald guided us to a small storeroom. "Get in," he commanded.

We stumbled into the **DARK ROOM** and Gerald slammed the door, locking it behind us.

"I will sign on your behalf tomorrow," Gerald said through the door. "And once Ari returns, he will confirm my decision while you three rot in here forever!"

We heard Gerald **LAUGHING** maniacally as he left the factory. We were completely trapped.

We **BANGED** on the heavy metal doors frantically, but our thuds just echoed through the empty factory. And with the sun now set, the room was almost completely black.

There was **NOTHING** we could do.

MONDAY MORNING — VERY EARLY

I awoke to the cold stone floor beneath my head.

UGH!

Zeke, Jez and I had been stuck in the factory storeroom overnight. We had eventually decided that it was too dark to do anything, and we were better off just sleeping.

But now it was morning and

there was light peeking through
a skylight, high above our heads—
wait . . . we hadn't seen that last
night!

"Dudes!" I hissed at my friends.

Jez and Zeke stirred.

"Look!" I said, pointing to the ceiling.
"There's light coming through.
I reckon we can **ESCAPE**
through that skylight."

"But how do we get up there?"
Jez asked, rubbing sleep from her
eyes.

"Zeke," I said, getting an idea. "In my world, you are an **OBBY KING.** Are you a pro in your world, too?"

"He sure is," Jez grinned.

"Think you can run up the wall and grab onto those **CEILING PIPES?"** I said, pointing above us. "Then move along until you get to the skylight and **KICK** it open?"

Zeke looked at the wall. "I dunno, mate. It's pretty high. But I'll give it a go."

Zeke took a run up. He pumped
his legs up the wall, but at about
halfway, he fell back down.

"This room is too small! I need a
bigger run up," he complained.

"You can do it, Zeke," Jez
encouraged.

Zeke tried again and fell.

I looked down, disappointed. Then
I realized what I was wearing.

"AIR PUMP 3000s! Put
these on!" I said, tearing them off

my feet. "They'll give you heaps of extra lift."

Zeke and I swapped shoes. I held my breath. He **BOLTED** towards the wall and ran up it at speed. It was like his feet were flying! Zeke reached his arms up high and grabbed the pipe.

Then he **SWUNG** like a chimpanzee, arm over arm, moving towards the skylight. Once he reached it, he swung his legs up hard and kicked it open.

"YEAH!" we cheered.

"What's up there?" Jez yelled.

"Looks like I'm on the roof," Zeke called down. "But it's really **HIGH.** I can't jump down—I'd break into a million blocks."

Now how were we going to get out of here?

"WAIT!" Zeke yelled, disappearing from view. After a minute, Zeke came back and threw down a rope.

"Where'd you find that?!" I called up to him.

"It was holding up a shade cloth," Zeke replied. He then secured one end of the rope to a metal drum, then threw the other end down to us. "Quick, **CLIMB UP!**"

Jez and I climbed. By the time I got to the top, my arms ached.

"Whoa! This is high," Jez breathed.

She was right. It was **WAY HIGHER** than I thought it would be. And there were no stairs on the outside of the building to help us down.

"Now what?" Zeke said, scratching his head.

We sat down, deflated.

But then I heard a light tinkling sound. I looked to the ground to see that something had fallen out of my pocket.

It was the dragon whistle!

I'd read that dragons had pretty good hearing, but could they hear me from miles away?

I stood up, took in a big breath and **BLEW HARD** into the whistle. I did this several times, then waited.

Then, a small shape appeared on the horizon. I watched as it got bigger. And bigger.

"It's a **DRAGON!**" Jez yelled.

The dragon from Other-Ari's estate came soaring through the clouds and landed gently on the roof.

"That's my girl!" I said, patting the dragon's head. She **PURRED.** "Can you give us a ride?"

The dragon snorted and turned so we could climb onto her back.

"Are you sure about this, mate?" Zeke asked nervously.

I nodded confidently. **"LET'S GO!"**

The dragon rose into the air and Zeke, Jez and I held on for dear life. She swooped and turned and corkscrewed through the air, making us all scream with terror and delight. She ducked and weaved around buildings and under bridges.

"WOOOOO-HOOOOOO!"

MONDAY—
A BIT LATER

"THERE!" Jez yelled, pointing to a crowd of people below.

All of the townspeople had gathered in an outdoor courtyard.

"Land there!" I directed the dragon.

Once the dragon landed, we **LEAPED** off her back and raced over to the crowd. The avatars were shocked and scared to see a dragon **CRASH** their meeting.

"STOP!" I yelled.

"What—how?!" Gerald yelled, standing up in alarm.

The Mayor of Blockville held a pen in her hand. "Oh, Ari, you're here," she said sadly. "Gerald was just about to **SIGN** on your behalf. My half has already been signed, which will hand Blockville over to your company. And then Gerald will finally be able to sell it to the factories."

She looked like she was about to cry.

"NO!" I said forcefully. "I don't agree to it. I'm not selling Blockville!"

Some business avatars among the crowd stood up, enraged. Gerald's face was hot with **ANGER.**

"You **WILL** sell," he commanded.

"No, I won't!" I said defiantly. I then **GRABBED** the contract and tore it up.

"And do you know what else? I'm removing all my money from your company. All the money I made that you put in my name to cover up your dirty deals. Well, the joke's on you, because that money is legally **MINE.** I'm going to use it to get Blockville back on its feet. And **DESTROY** your dirty company!"

The mayor's eyes glistened with joy.

"You can't do this!" Gerald **YELLED.** He glanced over to the business avatars with fear in his eyes.

"It's over, Gerald. You're **FINISHED**," I said.

Jez and Zeke ran in and **HUGGED** me. "Feel like coming over for a waterslide and more dragon flying?" I asked.

My friends **HIGH-FIVED.**

TUESDAY—
MIDDAY

I'd woken up on Tuesday morning
feeling anxious and excited.
Excited because I was going home.
Anxious because I had no idea
what Other-Ari would do once
he found out I'd taken all his
MONEY out of the company.

I'd organized to meet Other-Jez
and Zeke by the old park again
so they could come to the portal
with me. Once we met there, we
walked over to the portal, which

was **SHIMMERING** in the shadows.

Linking our arms, we dived through the portal together.

"WHOA!" Zeke and Jez yelled when they saw . . . Zeke and Jez!

I ran over to my friends from my world and pulled them into a hug. "I missed you guys **SO MUCH!"**

"Hey, what are those traitors doing here?" Other-Ari yelled at his Zeke and Jez.

"WAIT," I said, pulling Other-Ari

back. "Mate, you've been tricked and betrayed. Not by these guys, but by Gerald and his company. He lied to you and planned to sell Blockville to the factories to destroy the town! Jez and Zeke have been trying to contact you for months. And your family haven't abandoned you—they **WANT** to see you!"

"They do? I thought everyone **HATED** me," Other-Ari said sadly.

"No, that's only what Gerald told you. It's not true!" I promised.

"We've got a **LOT** to catch up on, mate," the Other-Zeke said.

"Well then, let's go!" Other-Ari said, and the three avatars leapd back through the portal.

As they disappeared through the shimmering purple haze, the portal flickered then faded to nothing, locking their world away from ours.

"Man, that was an epic few days," Zeke said.

"You have no idea," I laughed. I'd never been so happy to see my REAL FRIENDS.

"By the way," Jez said. "I don't think the Other-Ari has been to school in a while."

"Yeah, he closed the school over